JOSHUA STRAUB, PH.D.

Published by The Connextion Group, Nashville, TN

Cover Design © Micah Kandros Design

Typesetting: Micah Kandros Design

Video production: Change Media, Franklin, TN

Portions of this study are excerpted with permission from the book, *Safe House: How Emotional Safety is the Key to Raising Kids Who Live, Love and Lead Well*, by Joshua Straub, © 2015 Joshua Straub. All rights reserved. Published by Waterbrook Multnomah, Colorado Springs, CO.

This title may be purchased in bulk for educational, business, fundraising, or sales promotional use. For information, please e-mail josh@joshuastraub.com.

Unless otherwise noted, Scripture quotations are taken from the ENGLISH STANDARD VERSION. © 2001 by Crossway Bibles, a division of Good News Publishers. Scripture verses marked MSG are taken from THE MESSAGE. © 2002 by Eugene Peterson. Scripture verses marked NIV are taken from the NEW INTERNATIONAL VERSION. © 1984 by Zondervan.

CONTENTS

THE BLUEPRINT: GETTING STARTED

blue · print [ˈblo͞o,print][1]

noun
1. a design plan or other technical drawing

verb
1. draw up (a plan or model)

Building a house begins with the blueprint—a drawing or design plan of what we want the end result to look like. Without a plan, we're more likely to end up with a structure we never intended.

The same can be said for parenting. Without a plan, our children can too easily be raised up, not by the design we have for them but, instead, by the blueprint of a culture seeking to win their hearts, minds and souls.

What I love about the word blueprint is that it's also a verb.

Are you "blueprinting" a plan for your kids?

What does your "blueprinted" design for your kids look like?

What are the "blueprinted" outcomes you desire for your kids when they reach adulthood?

Building a Safe House requires a blueprint. Think of this study as your "how to" guide for "blueprinting" your Safe House.

There is one goal for this video study: **to help you put a plan in place that will make your home the emotionally and spiritually safest place on the planet for your kids.** Whether you're going through the study alone, with your spouse or in a small group, our desire is to help you set up an environment that leads your kids to emotional and relational abundance as adults.

"The plans of the diligent lead surely to abundance,
but everyone who is hasty comes only to poverty."
Proverbs 21:5, ESV

STUDY STRUCTURE

Each lesson has five parts:

Introduction: The introduction includes a story, quotations from the Safe House book (Waterbrook Multnomah, 2015), and a few questions to help prepare you for the video content.

Video Journal: As you watch the videos, take notes. Use the outline and space provided to also journal your personal interaction with the content.

You are the Safe House: The heart behind Safe House is first for you, the parent. These questions and discussion starters are meant to reassure and help you become a more secure parent, minus shame.

Within the Four Walls: An emotionally and spiritually safe home balances four walls over time: exploration, protection, grace and truth. These questions and discussion starters are meant to encourage and equip you in connecting at deeper levels with your children.

Becoming Safe: The application section of the study provides creative, fun and proven ways to build emotional safety with your kids.

STUDY DESIGN

The more investment you put into a study, the more you are likely to get out of it. However, you're a parent, so time and sleep are most likely hot commodities these days.

Though the study is broken into six lessons with an introduction, don't pressure yourself to complete it in six weeks. On the other hand, you may be the type of person who needs the structure to stay committed. Talk with your spouse or group about how you can get the most out of this study together.

Here are a few suggestions:

1. Don't try to digest everything in one sitting. Allow yourself small blocks of time throughout the week to journal, answer questions, and apply the principles. Finding large chunks of time as a parent is often impossible.

2. If you're meeting with your spouse or in a group, prepare yourself ahead of time by reading the introduction to that week's lesson.

3. To maximize your group's time together, you may decide to watch the video individually before convening as a group.

4. Don't dominate the discussion or allow any one individual to control the time together. If somebody in the group discovers he/she needs further counsel beyond what the group can offer, consult with your church to refer that individual to a safe counselor.

5. Discuss the You are the *Safe House* and *Within the Four Walls* questions. After your group meets, individually take small chunks of time throughout the week and go deeper. You can write answers to the questions and/or interact with the *Video Journal*.

6. Talk with your spouse or group about ways you will begin to apply the principles. Though there are a number of action steps in each lesson, pick only one or two you most need to apply for that week. Begin each group time together discussing how well you did, following through with your action step(s).

ERECT THE FOUR WALLS OF A SAFE HOUSE IN YOUR GROUP

EXPLORATION: Being emotionally safe with our kids is very difficult without a community of adults we can be emotionally safe with as well. Erect a wall of exploration that allows parents to explore their own stories. This may include our relationships with our parents, struggles with our spouses, the pros and cons of being a stay-at-home or working parent, or the travails of being a single parent. Exploration also includes brainstorming new ideas, activities and outside-the-box thinking for how parents can become more emotionally connected with their kids.

PROTECTION: Emotional safety begins with confidentiality. Erect a wall of protection around your group so that no stories leave the group.

"Show hospitality to one another without grumbling. As each has received a gift, use it to serve one another, as good stewards of God's varied grace."
1 Peter 4:9-10, ESV

GRACE: Sometimes our stories are filled with brokenness. Be a steward of God's grace with those in your group who are broken. If you are the one who is broken, be gracious to those who have caused your hurt. Your group should be a safe place to help bring healing to *your* story, not to disparage or gossip about somebody else's.

TRUTH: The principles of Safe House are grounded in scientific research and filtered through the lens of the Bible. Parenting advice is a dime a dozen. Don't be the group that throws around unsolicited or groundless advice. Always use Scripture as your foundation for Truth.

THE SCIENCE OF EMOTIONAL SAFETY

You may focus quite a bit of money, time, and energy on the physical safety of your kids—BPA-free products, electrical outlet covers, gluten-free diets, etc. We do. But have you ever considered the outcomes of emotional safety? The marketplace is relatively silent on it because there are no products on a shelf that can provide emotional safety the way you—mom and dad—can. As you go through the study, consider that emotional safety is related to outcomes in the following areas (all specifically listed in chapter 3 of *Safe House*, Waterbrook Multnomah, 2015):

- ~ children's academic scores
- ~ behaviors
- ~ brain development
- ~ social skills
- ~ problem-solving skills
- ~ relationship formation
- ~ adult-relationship satisfaction
- ~ healthy identity formation
- ~ self-esteem
- ~ athletic and extracurricular success
- ~ a sense of morality
- ~ established values
- ~ a faith that sticks

You won't find either the breadth or depth of outcome research for kids in any other parenting philosophy or strategy. Simply put, emotional safety is the key to raising kids who thrive in all areas of life—kids less likely to rebel, lie, and use drugs in their teenage years. Most importantly, we can raise kids who love God, love others, and lead others to do the same. All it takes is a place of emotional safety—or a Safe House.

What good is it if we have a child who never gets a scratch, bump, or bruise;

was fully breast-fed; and is as healthy as they come, never being sick and always eating organic vegetables, if he/she is a narcissistic, self-centered, irrational and, perhaps, impulsive and addicted brat who blames, criticizes, and is otherwise unloving? Or if he/she is a child who eventually becomes an adult unable to engage in intimate relationships or know the joy of sharing such a beautiful bond? Okay, that analogy may sound dramatic, but if my kids possess any of those traits, I'll be very sad. I'll take broken bones any day over a broken soul.

In order to raise children who love God and others, do well in school, excel in extracurricular activities, handle anger and frustration, develop self-control, resolve conflict, establish a good career, give back to the communities in which they live, and marry and raise their own families to do the same, we need to begin emphasizing more debate and added discussion in securing our homes emotionally. That's because emotionally safe homes are the breeding ground for kids who live, love, and lead well.

Emotional safety becomes the filter for all other parenting decisions. If there's any one phrase you take away from Safe House, remember this:

"It is the posture from which we parent, not the technique, that matters most."
Safe House (Waterbrook Multnomah, p. 12)

It really is that simple. Not easy. But simple.

(Excerpted from *Safe House*, Waterbrook Multnomah, p. 12)

ONE FINAL PLAN

Many parenting books and resources often leave parents filled with shame. If you're convicted by the Holy Spirit for something you did wrong, that's one thing, but living in constant shame as a parent doesn't come from the Holy Spirit… it comes from the enemy.

As parents living in the trenches, we know firsthand that more shame is not what we need to become better parents. Instead, we need a community of parents who come together to support one another in an effort to raise a generation of kids who live, love and lead well.

As you go throughout this study, remove shame from your group. Deal thoroughly with sin, but let forgiveness become the healing salve of being an imperfect parent. In this way, you'll not only teach your kids that they don't have to be perfect, but you'll also show them how to handle it when they're not.

To come together as parents in this endeavor, join with us in using #shamelessparenting and #SafeHouseFamily across social media outlets. Let's share ideas, laughs and, most importantly, support one another in raising a generation of kids in a #SafeHouseFamily.

"As parents feel for their children, God feels for those who fear him. He doesn't endlessly nag or scold, nor hold grudges forever. He doesn't treat us as our sins deserve, nor pay us back in full for our wrongs."
Psalm 103:13, 9-10, MSG

WHAT DO YOU HOPE TO GET OUT OF THIS STUDY?

_____

_____

_____

_____

LAYING THE FOUNDATION: WITH JOSH AND CHRISTI

INTRODUCTION

"I wanted to call this study 'the insecure parent' because it's something I've struggled with from day one." — Christi Straub

Here's the truth behind my wife's honest confession—she came from an emotionally safe home herself! Yet, fighting insecurity is still an ongoing struggle even for her. Just imagine coming into this parenting journey from a childhood that was not emotionally safe. Perhaps that's you.

My insecurity lies in trying to filter through all of the parenting advice constantly thrown my way. It's no wonder we're insecure as parents—there are a million voices telling us what to do that leave us constantly questioning our every parenting move.

As journalist, Eric Sevareid, wrote in 1964, "The biggest big business in America is not steel, automobiles, or television. It is the manufacture, refinement, and distribution of anxiety." Nowhere is this more true than in the marketplace of modern-day parenting.

Whether or not you came from an emotionally safe home, feeling insecure as a parent is very common. So let's begin there—as insecure parents coming together to support one another in becoming more secure for our kids. We're in this together!

When do you feel most alone as a parent?

_____

_____

_____

_____

What makes you feel most insecure as a parent? Comparing yourself to other parents? When your child constantly disobeys? When you yell, scream or manipulate your child into compliance?

_____

_____

_____

_____

Or perhaps the question for you is who makes you feel most insecure as a parent? Does your mom or dad correct your every parenting move? Is it a sibling? A group of friends? Random strangers who confront you in public?

_____

_____

_____

Who do you turn to in your feelings of insecurity? Your spouse? Your parents? Church family? A group of other parents/friends? God? Where do you tend to regain security as a parent?

_____

_____

_____

 **VIDEO JOURNAL**

For Christi, as a Type A, perfectionistic parent, she found hope in the idea of Safe House because it simplified the confusion.

Christi also mentioned there was an ugliness about her she didn't know existed until she became a parent.

One of the most encouraging and perspective-changing moments for Christi was when her mum told her, "God picked *you* to raise those children. He entrusted you with those precious little hearts."

We need community. We were not made to do this alone.

> "... For he knows the secrets of the heart. Search me, O God, and know my heart! Try me and know my thoughts! Create in me a clean heart, O God, and renew a right spirit within me."
>
> Psalm 44:21b; 139:23; 51:10, ESV

YOU ARE THE SAFE HOUSE: QUESTIONS FOR YOU

Have you experienced your "ugliness" more since becoming a parent? As we'll learn, everybody looks normal until we hit stress or duress. When kids arrive, there are new stressors placed on us we didn't have before, which can bring out more heart issues we didn't know existed. What about who you are or how you began to treat people (particularly your spouse) was surprising once you became parents (especially when multiple kids entered the picture)?

_____

_____

_____

_____

Do you find yourself speaking in a harsher tone to your spouse than you would to a stranger, especially in stressful moments? Write down your triggers. When do you become most overwhelmed? When does your "ugly" come out the most? If you are really brave, and spouses please be gentle here, ask your spouse when he/she sees or feels it the most.

_____

_____

_____

_____

"God picked *you* to raise those children. He entrusted *you* with those precious little hearts." Does this statement excite you? Scare you? Give you hope? Change your perspective? Discuss with your spouse or group what this truth means to you. How does it change how you look at yourself as a parent?

_____

_____

_____

_____

Moses, in Deuteronomy 6, in a speech he delivered about how to pass on a legacy through the generations, begins by saying, "Hear, O Israel." Read Deuteronomy 6:4-9 together. Many times we interpret this passage as if Moses was only talking to parents. He, instead, addresses the nation of Israel… or if he was giving this speech today, it would address the entire church.

_____

_____

_____

_____

We are not designed to parent alone. Rather, healthy parenting is best done in the context of a safe church community. How well do you embrace a support network around you to help as you raise your children? On a scale of 1 to 10, how well connected are you to your church family?

_____

_____

_____

_____

Do you have trouble asking others for help? If so, what hinders that number from being higher? Insecurity? Fear? Anxiety? Expectations? Time? Exhaustion?

_____

_____

_____

Write down, in order of who you turn to most often, the five emotionally and spiritually safest people in your life right now. How often do you turn to them for help, counsel or simply to hang out?

_____

_____

_____

Who can walk with you as you take the necessary steps to becoming more secure as a parent?

_____

_____

_____

_____

"Hear, O Israel... love the Lord your God with all your heart...
teach [my commands] diligently to your children."
Deuteronomy 6:4-7, ESV (abbreviated)

WITHIN THE FOUR WALLS: QUESTIONS RELATED TO YOUR KIDS

Describe what your "ugly" looks like toward your kids.

_____

_____

_____

_____

When is your "ugly" most triggered in relation to your kids? Is it a particular behavior expressed by your child? Time of day? Situation? Event?

_____

_____

_____

_____

"For the whole law is fulfilled in one word: 'You shall love your neighbor as yourself.'"
Galatians 5:14, ESV

The way we treat others is often reflective of how we see ourselves. The Bible says, "... you shall love your neighbor as yourself." What is implied here? Do you believe your insecurity as a parent is connected to how you treat your kids, particularly in those "ugly" moments?

_____

_____

_____

_____

What are some ways you can apply grace in your relationship with your kids, beginning with yourself?

_____

_____

_____

_____

How does realizing that God chose *you* as the mommy or daddy of your precious children change how you see them? How do you think it will change how you interact with them?

_____

_____

_____

_____

Write down the five emotionally and spiritually safest people in your child's life right now. How often do they spend time with them? In what context?

_____

_____

_____

_____

BECOMING SAFE: APPLICATION

✔ In Matthew 6:9-13, Jesus gives us instruction on how to pray. Read the following abbreviation and minor paraphrase of this prayer aloud:

"Father, let your kingdom come, let your will be done, on earth as it is in heaven."
Matthew 6:9-10, ESV

Imagine now the moments you feel the most shame as a parent. Picture your most embarrassing moments or parenting mess ups. Now reread the following passage:

"As parents feel for their children, God feels for those who fear him. He doesn't endlessly nag or scold, nor hold grudges forever. He doesn't treat us as our sins

deserve, nor pay us back in full for our wrongs."
Psalm 103:13, 9-10, MSG

In praying the Lord's Prayer, have you ever thought about it in relation to how we relate to one another? *"Father, let the way you relate in your kingdom be done on earth as it is heaven."* Shame, embarrassment and ridicule are not the Father's way of relating.

✔ If you are living in shame or insecurity as a parent, ask the group to help you experience the love of the Father as read in Psalm 103. Take each day this coming week and pray through Psalm 103 every morning before everyone else in the house is awake. Post this verse on your refrigerator, dashboard or bathroom mirror.

✔ Living in shame and insecurity is one thing... being convicted about sinful behavior is another. If you or someone in your group are convicted about a sinful behavior toward your child, that person needs to apologize and take time for safe confession, forgiveness and repentance. If the group is safe enough, or you and your spouse feel secure in doing so, surround one another in love and pray for forgiveness. Then, find someone in your group or list of emotionally and spiritually safe people to walk with you in an effort to refrain from this behavior.

✔ God chose you to raise your kids. Imagine Jesus playing with your kids in the backyard, jumping on the trampoline, going down the slide, having a tea party or putting puzzles together. Take one hour this week and enter your child's world. Play in the backyard as a friend. Allow your children to lead the play. Let them decide what you do together during that one hour. Afterward, write down observations about them and their hearts you either hadn't noticed before or cherished about who they are.

✔ If you're feeling alone as a parent or finding community is an area of growth for you, find one person, or a couple, in your church or circle of friends you and your spouse can reach out to this week to begin getting more connected. Meet at a restaurant, have them over to your house, or get together at a park with the kids.

✔ Remember to use #SafeHouseFamily and #shamelessparenting to connect in our virtual community of ideas. What's working for you? What's not working? Did another mom drop by to take your kids for a drive so you could get a break? Did another family bring you a meal? Show us your parenting wins. Oh yeah, share some laughs too. Everybody knows we could all use some gut-wrenching laughter.

LESSON ONE:
SAFE RELATIONSHIP = LOVE-FEAR

INTRODUCTION

Our homes reflect our stories. For some, the story is defined by brokenness. For others, it's defined by love, laughter, and joy. For most, it's a blend of each.

The beauty of it all is that no matter our story or family background—good, bad or ugly—we have 100% control in writing a new script. And it's a good thing, too. Research shows that, as parents, we're the ones writing our children's stories—and wiring their brains as well.

That's because from the very moment our children are born, they're asking questions. Am I important? Am I wanted? Am I needed? Am I loved? These questions can be merged into one primary question, "Am I safe?" Whether we recognize it or not, we're answering that question by how we interact with our kids each day, particularly in their stressful moments when they need us most.

That's both a powerful and scary realization. Especially considering that most of us parent the way our parents raised us, for better or for worse, oftentimes without even realizing it.

Have you ever considered what kind of story you're writing for your children? Or what effect your story is having on those little ones you love most? It's a story we'll begin writing down.

Describe or write down in your own words what *emotional safety* means to you.

_____

_____

_____

_____

Read 1 John 4:18-19. Write down three observations you initially make about this passage.

"There is no fear in love, but perfect love casts out fear. For fear has to do with punishment, and whoever fears has not been perfected in love. We love because he first loved us."
1 John 4:18-19, ESV

1. _____

2. _____

3. _____

"A Safe House is not just a place, it's a relationship. You are the Safe House. To your children, you are home."
Safe House (Waterbrook Multnomah, p. 25)

 **VIDEO JOURNAL**

Our kids have emotional bullets coming at them every day. That's why our homes should be the emotionally safest place in the world for our kids.

Our ability to be secure in our own stories matters for how emotionally present we can be with our kids when they need us most.

The foundation of a Safe House is a secure parent. Central to our security as parents is our ability to speak or have written our own narrative.

Nar · ra · tive
noun
a spoken or written account of connected events; a story

The foundation of a Safe House is a secure parent.

The framework of a Safe House is understanding.
"In order to be understood, we must first understand."
Safe House (Waterbrook Multnomah, p. 56)

The four walls of a Safe House are exploration, protection, grace and truth.

Balancing the four walls over time is a function of how well we understand the underlying motivation of our children's behavior, temperament, cognitive skill development and situation.

Understanding is a function of how secure we are as parents.

Safe Relationship = Love – Fear

THE BIBLE: *"There is no fear in love, but perfect love casts out fear."*

1 John 4:18, ESV

SCIENCE: "… we need to be open to our child, feeling that safety in ourselves and creating that sense of *'love without fear'* in our child." [ii]

The same root for the word to describe the Father's "compassion" for us in Psalm 103 is found in the word, "yearn," in 1 Kings 3:26 (ESV) when "… the woman whose son was alive said to the king, because her heart *yearned* for her son, 'Oh, my lord, give her the living child, and by no means put him to death….'"

What does the understanding of God as a Father in this light mean to you?

_____

_____

_____

_____

"Unless the Lord builds the house, those who build it labor in vain."
Psalm 127:1, ESV

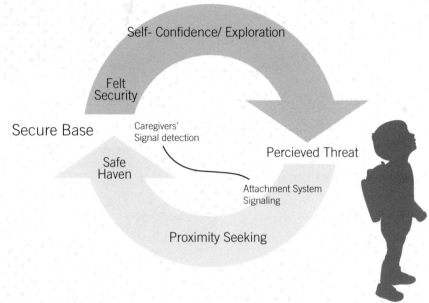

Figure 1. The Circle of Security [iii]

Our kids use us as a secure base and need us to support their exploration. This exploration leads to self-confidence later in life. As our children explore, they need us to delight in them, enjoy their presence and help them.

But what happens when they explore too far and encounter a real or perceived threat? They signal back to us to get our attention. This is when **they need us** to welcome them, especially in the face of the fearful threat. The primary reason is that our children don't know what to do with their overwhelmed feelings.

Our ability to be a safe haven when they seek us for protection and comfort in those stressful moments is the setting children need for a beautiful story. They need us to remain calm, take charge of the situation, and stay with them until we understand the underlying feeling that is too much for them to be alone. As this safe haven, we help our children learn to organize their feelings. **This is why the posture from which we parent matters more than the techniques.**

What were your thoughts about the ending story used to describe the posture of emotional safety? How would you have reacted?

YOU ARE THE SAFE HOUSE: QUESTIONS FOR YOU

> *"Your testimonies are my heritage forever, for they are the joy of my heart."*
> Psalm 119:111, ESV

We're going to begin discussing your story. As you answer the questions throughout this particular section in each lesson, journal your thoughts and behaviors as a parent and see if you can make connections to how you were raised. If these exercises bring up too much pain, give yourself grace and take your time. It is always best to do these type of exercises in the presence and safety of others you trust. If you or someone in your group need to connect further with a professional counselor, be sure to consult with your local church or see the list of contacts in the appendix for a referral in your local area.

What are two ways your mom was not emotionally safe for you?

_____

_____

What are two ways your mom was emotionally safe for you?

_____

_____

What are two ways your dad was not emotionally safe for you?

_____

_____

What are two ways your dad was emotionally safe for you?

_____

_____

What connections, both healthy and unhealthy, do you see between the way you treat your kids and the way your parents treated you?

_____

_____

Write about or discuss a rupture you had with your parent(s) in the past. Was it resolved? What was that process like?

_____

_____

Think of the fearful ways we *react* to our kids in stressful moments when they act out. Yelling. Blaming. Punishing. Shaming. Maybe even spanking out of anger.

These *reactions* in such overwhelming moments tend to be fear-based. Look at the last part of 1 John 4:18: "… For fear has to do with punishment, and whoever fears has not been perfected in love."

When we *react* to our kids out of the insecurities from our own stories, we do so from fear—fear of our kids turning out a certain way, fear of treating our kids the way our parents treated us, fear of losing control as a parent, or perhaps even fear of being seen as a bad parent. *Reacting* out of fear often leads to *punishing* our kids for their behavior in these moments rather than disciplining them, a difference we'll get to later. For now, it's important to understand that reacting out of fear usually places the primary focus on our kids' behavior before the relationship.

When we as parents react to our kids out of fear, it's not their misbehavior our kids are thinking about, it's the fear of disconnection they feel from the person who is supposed to be the emotionally safest in their life. [iv] This is how the tendency to recreate the cycle of fear is rooted in our own stories.

(Excerpt taken from *Safe House*, Waterbrook Multnomah, p. 20)

What are some of the fears you have that impact how you interact with your kids? Even just voicing those fears, or writing them down, can often take the power out of them.

_____

_____

_____

_____

Is it easy or difficult to think about God as such a compassionate Father? Write about the ways you have seen or experienced Him "yearning" for you as a son/daughter.

_____

_____

_____

_____

With God as your secure base, describe a time you sought Him out after either exploring too far or experiencing danger? In what ways do you seek proximity to God in such moments? How would you describe how He responds to you as a safe haven? Write out five words that describe God in these moments.

_____

_____

*"God is our refuge and strength, a **very present** help in trouble."*
Psalm 46:1, ESV

WITHIN THE FOUR WALLS: QUESTIONS RELATED TO YOUR KIDS

What are the primary emotional bullets with which your kids are dealing? Difficult teacher? Pressure with grades? Sexual behaviors? Bullying at school? Online social relationships? Other?

_____

_____

_____

_____

What grade would you give yourself for how well, age-appropriately, you are allowing your kids to explore? Explain the grade you gave yourself.

_____

_____

_____

_____

In what ways have you found yourself being emotionally safe with your kids, particularly in stressful or threatening situations? Describe your responses.

_____

_____

_____

_____

Remember, those repeated, secure base interactions with our kids—when they experience us as a safe haven—teaches them what to expect and how to behave in relationships.

One my closest friends, who is both gifted at and loves starting businesses, regularly discusses micro- and macroeconomics with his 16-year-old son. Yes, his son is wicked smart. As the safe and present father that he is, my friend uses business projects to train his son for the real world.

Recently, while on a year-long mission in Costa Rica as a family, he decided to help his son earn money with a microfinancing project using an incredible woodworker from a local village. Not only would this project teach his son how to earn money, it would help the local economy as well.

As he told me about it, I could hear in his voice the excitement for his son. The further involved they got, the more passionate my friend became.

About a week later, my friend called me sounding unusually depressed. He said, "Josh, you know the project we've been working on? Well, my son looked at me and said, 'Dad, this is your project with my name on it. If you want me to learn, let me do something that I'm passionate about.'"

I asked my friend how he responded. He said they went for a walk along the beach and, after listening to his son's point of view, he looked at him and said, "You know, you're right. I'm sorry."

My friend continued, "I asked him what he wanted to do. No rules applied. He told me he wanted to build a space hotel. So that's where we started."

What my friend realized was that even though his intentions were so incredibly good-willed, he actually did his son a disservice by overstepping his bounds and quarterbacking the project for him.

"I went from teaching him a lesson to letting him watch a lesson," he concluded. "I realized how imperfect my actions can be, even though my intentions for my kids may be pure."

If you read the verse in 1 John and were left with the lingering thought in your mind, All of this perfect love and 'parenting without fear' stuff is great, but I am not God, that's right where you need to be.

If we try to be perfect, we'll parent out of fear.

If we think we should never make a mistake, we'll make parenting choices out of fear.

If we ebb and flow with the latest parenting technique and strategy, choosing to give timeouts this week and not the next, we'll parent out of fear.

So let yourself off of the hook now… you won't parent perfectly. You won't love your kids perfectly either. You are not God. Neither am I. Like you, I'm an imperfect parent trying to do the best I can to raise my kids to live, love, and lead well.

We will lose our tempers.

We will say things we regret.

Our parental agendas will get in the way of what's best for our kids.

Isn't that awesome? We're all on this journey of imperfection together. Now, repeat aloud after me and admit to yourself:

Parenting is hard. I am not God. I am not perfect. I will make mistakes. I don't need to get it right all the time. I just need to be safe.

In fact, choosing to be an imperfect parent is choosing to be a safe parent. Research shows that emotionally safe parents, if they can emotion coach their kids just 40% of the time, are doing well. (Emotion coaching is a technique covered in lesson 5 of the study and chapter 8 of the *Safe House* book). So feel free to mess up. Why? Because research shows that "repair" is one of the greatest parenting strategies you have as a parent. [v]

What does the Bible say about this repair strategy researchers talk about? It calls it forgiveness. And it tells us to practice it—a lot.

By repairing a rupture in our relationship with our kids, we free them from any expectation to be perfect themselves. Not only that, it teaches our kids the appropriate way of handling imperfection when they make a mistake as well.

(Excerpt taken from *Safe House*, Waterbrook Multnomah, p. 21-22)

Based on the story Josh tells in the video of the dad and daughter who wanted to go to the football game, which parenting posture would be your tendency? Rate yourself on a scale of 1-10, 1 being that you pay no attention whatsoever to your kid's negative emotions and 10 being that you positively validate him/her.

BECOMING SAFE: APPLICATION

✔ Put a plan in place for resolving unforgiveness toward a parent. You may write that parent a letter and give it to your spouse. If reconciliation is needed, and possible, consider meeting with that parent to resolve the rupture… just don't harbor unforgiveness.

✔ To honor your parents, write a thank-you letter to them for the specific ways they were emotionally available to you.

✔ Write down one behavior of yours that's making your home emotionally unsafe for your kids. Discuss with your spouse or group a plan for how you will decrease that behavior this week. What will, instead, be your emotionally safe response?

✔ Depending on the age of your children, sit down with them this week and memorize 1 John 4:18 together. Ask your kids what it is about

your home, and your relationship with them, that makes them feel
emotionally safe.

✔ Again, depending on the age of your kids and quality of those
relationships, sit down with them this week and ask what "emotional
bullets" they feel most pressured by. Create a list. Then, beside each
"bullet," stressor or pressure, write a Bible verse that helps them think
differently about how they can handle it. Brainstorm with them and pray
about how you can be the emotional safe haven they need.

NOTES

NOTES

_____
_____
_____
_____
_____
_____
_____
_____
_____
_____
_____
_____
_____
_____
_____
_____
_____
_____
_____
_____
_____
_____
_____
_____
_____
_____
_____
_____
_____
_____

LESSON TWO:
BECOMING A SECURE PARENT

INTRODUCTION

PARENTING ISN'T ROCKET SCIENCE; IT'S JUST BRAIN SURGERY.

There's never a more important time to begin parenting from the foundation of a safe relationship than in the first year of life. By one year of age, how a child views relationships the rest of his/her life is pretty well established. How we parent, relate to, and respond to our children in times of fear and anxiety teaches them *from the day they're born* how relationships work.

My wife, Christi, wrote a blog post shortly after our son, Landon, was born. It was about a game we played with him called the Face Game. Babies love to stare at faces. When mom and dad make exaggerated faces, they watch intently and learn to respond with the same emotion. Silly faces make for joy-filled smiles and squeals. Serious faces make for frowns.

Also, babies are born with two innate fears: fear of falling and fear of loud noises. Every other fear in life is learned.

When Landon was about eight-months-old, I accidently dropped a pot in the kitchen, making an obnoxious, ear-piercing noise. Standing in his play gym right next to me, Landon immediately jumped. As his bottom lip started to quiver, he looked directly to his mom. What did she do? She smiled.

Her smile told Landon, "Baby boy, there is nothing to fear."

Landon smiled back. Peace was restored.

Our fun little Face Game with our kids goes far beyond the sweet squeals and giggly memories. The Face Game is literally wiring our children's brains. When Landon or Kennedy look at our faces and reflect our emotions, it changes the way their brains fire and wire.

When our children experience something startling—and potentially scary—their amygdala, the fear center (or bottom part) of their brains, starts firing. They look to us to see how to respond. When we respond with a smile, their brains translate: "Baby, there is nothing to fear." And there is an instant calming as the cerebral cortex tells the nervous system, "You can calm down."

It's called neural integration. But my wife calls it AWE-some.

The Face Game is one strategy for creating a Safe House, an environment that literally wires our children's brains for safe relationships. I want to point out the fantastic biblical connection my wife made while playing the Face Game with Landon. The spiritual parallels with God the Father, who gave the Israelites this blessing and promise, are pretty remarkable: *"The LORD bless you and keep you; the LORD make his face shine upon you and be gracious to you; the LORD turn his face toward you and give you peace"* (Numbers 6:24-26, NIV, emphasis added). In the devotional words of my wife:

When we gaze upon our Heavenly Father's face—he turns his face toward us, and gives us peace. True peace. Peace is just one intentional look away. He's waiting. I just have to turn toward it, rather than away from it.

And just because God is AWE-some, he allows us, as parents, to share in a little bit of his joy. We give our babies peace when they gaze at our face. Just as our Heavenly Father does for us. How neat is that?

When things are startling and stressful in my life, instead of reacting with anxiety or panic, what if I gazed into my Father's face? I know I would see his smile. His smile would tell me, "Baby girl, there is nothing to fear."

The Bible says, *"Unless the LORD builds the house, those who build it labor in vain"* (Psalm 127:1, ESV). The peaceful home is a home where we as parents are turning to God in our own fears. As we do, no matter how stressful life or parenting gets, we communicate to our kids that God himself is safe, and in him, there is nothing to fear. Because perfect love drives out fear (1 John 4:18).

(Excerpted from *Safe House*, Waterbrook Multnomah, p. 23-24)

VIDEO JOURNAL

Going back to the circle of security—your child's repeated interaction with you as a secure base, where he/she experiences you as a safe haven—creates for him/her an internalized model of relationships that carries forward to new relationship experiences. This is how our children learn **what to expect** and **how to behave** in close relationships.

Our children's core beliefs about relationships are developed as implicit memories. Think of tying your shoe. You don't have to consciously think about how you tie the knots. The action is implicit, or instinctual. The same idea holds true for how we learn to relate to others.

Explicit memories, on the other hand, require conscious attention. Where implicit memory is present at birth, explicit memory begins to develop around the second year of life. The goal in writing or talking about your own story is that you are recalling "explicitly" factual and autobiographic events that may, otherwise, remain unconscious to you.

Your "narrative," therefore, is your ability to "explicitly" piece together relationship events from your childhood that bring meaning to how you relate to your children (and spouse).

When we put language (left brain) to these relationship events (right brain), we "bind the book" of our brains, if you will, to connect why we believe, act, and feel the way we do in close intimate relationships.

The coherency of our stories impacts how safe we are with our kids. Our inability to understand our children's underlying feelings and needs could mean we punish, minimize, or dismiss their overwhelming emotions.

Relationship Styles:
(For more detailed descriptions, see p. 36-38 of *Safe House*, Waterbrook Multnomah, 2015.)

Secure: Comfortable with intimacy and autonomy

Avoidant: Avoidant of intimacy, overly autonomous

Anxious: Anxious about abandonment, overly clingy

Being emotionally present with another individual requires the executive skills of the brain we want to develop in our children, beginning with emotion regulation.

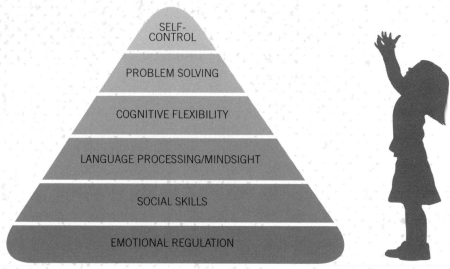

Figure 2. Pyramid of Self-control

(For a more detailed list and description of the higher-level brain skills developed in a Safe House, see p. 65-66 of Safe House, Waterbrook Multnomah, 2015.)

This is how we become brain surgeons for our kids... by simply being emotionally safe.

REWRITING YOUR STORY

1. Remember Your Story – Recall your story through journaling, meeting with your spouse or small group, and answering the questions throughout this study.

You were not meant to go through this healing journey alone. Build your Safe Life Team around you. If you need professional counseling, please contact your local church or see the list of counseling directories in the appendix for a referral.

2. Recognize Unresolved Hurt – Be honest about events or relationship ruptures that have gone unaddressed or were easier to bury.

3. Reframe the Meaning of Your Story – Be sure to invite God into this process. Reframing means we look deeper into events. Many of us assume blame for a parent's divorce or the way we were treated, when the reality is the responsibility was on the one who hurt us, intentional or unintentional.

4. Redeem Your Story – Forgive. Be a steward of God's varied grace to your parents (or those who hurt you). Accept the hurt in light of God's grace and for how He is redeeming your story.

5. Reconnect – Strengthen emotional strings of safety, trust and intimacy with others. If reconciliation is possible, seek that out in due time. Accept influence from others.

> *"… It is **not good** that the man should be **alone**…."*
> Genesis 2:18, ESV

YOU ARE THE SAFE HOUSE: QUESTIONS FOR YOU

Rewrite the five words you wrote in the last section to describe God as a safe haven. Describe what your behaviors, actions, and words would look like if you parented in the same way.

Where would you place yourself on the following continuum as it relates to your relationship style?

Anxious over abandonment   Secure   Avoidant of intimacy

○————————————————————————————○

Where would your spouse place you?

○————————————————————————————○

Anxious over abandonment   Secure   Avoidant of intimacy

Remember, these are our relationship tendencies when we're in stress or not feeling safe. When, in your marriage, do you not feel safe? Using the circle of security for your marriage, what triggers your attachment system?

_____

_____

_____

Do you tend to withdraw, become clingy, or seek closeness to your spouse in a healthy way when feeling threatened by an external (job issues, money problems, kids, etc.) or internal (feeling insecure, lonely, disrespected, angry) trigger?

_____

_____

_____

Describe how you are a safe haven for your spouse when he/she is under duress. What behaviors, actions, and words most comfort your spouse?

_____

_____

_____

_____

On a scale of 1 to 10, 1 being very few words on the page and 10 being a completed book, how would you describe the coherency of your story? What are your next steps?

_____

_____

_____

_____

WITHIN THE FOUR WALLS: QUESTIONS RELATED TO YOUR KIDS

> *"My child isn't giving me a hard time. My child is having a hard time."* [vi]
> John Gottman

Of the cognitive skills described, which skills do each of your children most need to build?

_____

_____

_____

Of the cognitive skills described, which do you most need to build when interacting with your children?

_____

_____

Go back and read each of the temperaments (found on p. 60-61 of *Safe House*, Waterbrook Multnomah). Write down your child's unique temperaments.

_____

_____

_____

_____

Write your two biggest fears of changing how you parent now to parenting in a more emotionally present way. After you write those fears, answer this question: What's the worst that could happen?

_____

_____

_____

_____

In the moments you are completely overwhelmed and angry with your kids, write down and discuss two ways you can regulate your emotion and calm down before reacting to them in a negative way?

_____

_____

_____

_____

BECOMING SAFE: APPLICATION

✔ Create a genogram of your family. There is free software and guidelines for how to design a genogram at www.genopro.com. Use this to help find patterns in your family and see yourself in light of a much larger generational narrative.

✔ Spend some time reflecting in awe of who God is. He created us to relate and, when we relate well, our brains are wired to experience the joy of loving others. But He also designed us in a way that when we're broken (because of the fall of man), we can be healed in no other place than—relationships. Spend time journaling this week the relational moments that bring you the most joy.

✔ Every time you're overwhelmed or angry with your kids this week, journal how you reacted or responded. Apply the two ways you chose to regulate your emotion before approaching your child about his/her behavior or tantrum. Journal about your experience in doing this. Compare the outcome between when you *react* and when you *respond*.

✔ If you haven't already, begin the process of rewriting your story. Of course this isn't a perfectly linear process, so enter it where you are now and allow God to redeem it.

✔ Plan a date this week with your spouse. Use it to discuss how you can be more emotionally safe and present with one another. Don't blame or criticize. Simply spend time together describing how the other person makes you feel safe.

NOTES

NOTES

_____

_____

_____

_____

_____

_____

_____

_____

_____

_____

_____

_____

_____

_____

_____

_____

_____

_____

_____

_____

_____

_____

_____

_____

_____

_____

_____

LESSON THREE: BUILDING THE FOUR WALLS

INTRODUCTION

"Kids who feel understood are kids who learn to understand; kids who understand are kids who love."
Safe House (Waterbrook Multnomah, p. 55)

Choosing to seek the deeper understanding and meaning behind our child's behavior takes us beyond how she's behaving to a picture of why she's behaving that way. And the more we understand why, the more our kids feel understood and the more equipped we are to know how much grace to apply in a given situation, what limits to set, and how. In doing so, we can effectively build the brains of our children in a way that serves each child individually and uniquely based on their developmental level, temperament, and skill level.

Not only will we then be coauthors of beautiful stories for our children but artists with an eye for drawing out the innocence behind our kids' behaviors.

(Excerpted from *Safe House*, Waterbrook Multnomah, p. 55)

In piecing together your narrative, what insights are you gaining about yourself? God? Your spouse?

How have these exercises helped you see your children differently? How is it changing the way you respond to them in their most stressful moments?

VIDEO JOURNAL

In order to be understood, we must first understand.

The goal in raising our children is to move them from 100% dependence on us as infants to 100% independence (or interdependence) on us as adults. The balance of exploration and protection, age-appropriately, is critical.

Exploration is giving our child age-appropriate freedom to discover and interact with her world. In contrast, *protection* is ensuring her safety by stepping in to intervene when necessary, and being a consistent, loving presence for her to come back to as "home base." Striking a balance on the exploration-protection continuum is critically important to a child's emotional, psychological and spiritual development.

Overprotected children are robbed of the opportunity to develop healthy individuality and self-confidence because they are given few opportunities to tackle challenges and problem solve. *Overprotecting can actually hurt kids in the long run because we offer them little to no challenge.* [vii]

Some of us swing to the opposite extreme of giving our kids too much freedom—a term known as laissez-faire parenting. Laissez-faire is French, meaning "to let people do as they please." Parenting from this posture often means neglecting the wall of protection altogether *and running the risk of overwhelming our children of life's challenges too early for their emotional and age-appropriate development.*

(Excerpted from *Safe House*, Waterbrook Multnomah, p. 72-73)

The walls that sit between exploration and protection and across from one another are the walls of grace and truth. The wall of GRACE represents unconditional love of our children. To be true grace it cannot be earned but instead freely given. Grace is loving our children even when they are unlovable. Grace is supporting our children even, and especially, in their worst moments. Grace is understanding the feelings and motives behind our children's behavior. Grace is forgiving our kids when they wrong us. Grace is choosing not to disrespect our kids even when they disrespect us. Grace is helping our kids whenever they need us. The wall of grace is where our kids learn empathy. Critical to their development is our ability to understand and embrace their negative emotion, without judgment, even if it's directed at us.

The wall opposite of grace is *truth*. I use the word truth because it covers much more than just discipline or setting limits, though both fall along this wall. A child who lives in truth does the right thing. The wall of TRUTH takes into account the consequences of our actions, both good and bad. Truth is teaching our children about the values of hard work and responsibility. Truth is helping our children learn the value of discernment when making decisions. Truth is training our children to live with integrity. Truth is walking alongside our children as they learn how to respond to the bumps and bruises of life, like not making the football team. Truth is helping your 135-pound uncoordinated son realize he'll never play in the NFL.

(Excerpted from *Safe House*, Waterbrook Multnomah, p. 63)

Simply put, grace is loving and accepting our children for who they are; truth is loving them enough to not leave them that way.

The Truth Pathway
The truth pathway is absolutely telling our children what to do. "You'll do this because I'm the parent and I said so," this parent chides. "Case closed." Don't forget, you're the parent. There are times our children simply need to obey with zero negotiation. Particularly in instances of physical danger, potentially harmful situations, or if you're pressured for time, this pathway is unquestionably warranted.

I also love what my mother-in-law did. If any of her kids needed an immediate answer (i.e., permission for a sleepover), she would say, "If you need to know now, the answer is no." I use this principle even today as an adult. The point is, don't allow your kids to corner or manipulate you into a making an immediate decision.

The Grace Pathway
The grace pathway may very well, on certain days, save your sanity. "Go ahead and do it," this parent quips. There are times we need to temporarily drop our concern. This most often happens when we're worked up ourselves. To maintain the relationship with our children and not say or do something we regret, it's better to resort to this pathway than to ridicule, judge, blame or criticize.

Though there are times we need to instill absolute truth or definitive grace in parenting situations, the pathway that engages our children to think, feel, and relate at the same time and build their brains unites grace and truth:

The Safe House Pathway
"Your concern is wanting to stay out later with your friends. My concern is you have an exam tomorrow. Let's find a way to resolve this together," this parent responds. The most emotionally healthy, academically competent, and relation-

ally stable children have parents who are neither too lenient nor too strict. These parents set reasonable limits for their children, are warm and responsive, and do not use harsh methods of punishment. [viii]

(Excerpted from *Safe House*, Waterbrook Multnomah, p. 105-106)

Refer to Philippians 4:5-8. As parents, our ability to be present with our kids in their anxiety functions, in a finite way, as the peace they need to calm their fears and overwhelmed brains.

Only then can we begin to help them think about limits and consequences.

"… do not be anxious about anything, but in everything by prayer and supplication with thanksgiving let your requests be made known to God. And the peace of God, which surpasses all understanding, will guard your hearts and your minds in Christ Jesus.

Finally, brothers, whatever is true, whatever is honorable, whatever is just, whatever is pure, whatever is lovely, whatever is commendable, if there is any excellence, if there is anything worthy of praise, think about these things."
Philippians 4:6-8, ESV

YOU ARE THE SAFE HOUSE: QUESTIONS FOR YOU

Describe, specifically, how you were raised based on the four walls. What walls did your parents tend to parent from most often? For instance, were you coddled (grace) and protected (protection) with few rules (truth) and exploration? Or did your parents send you out to learn "the hard way?" Write about the walls they most emphasized.

_____

_____

_____

_____

How did it feel living under those walls? Do you wish your parents had emphasized one wall more? Describe your responses.

_____

_____

_____

_____

Describe the connection, as best you can, between the walls your parents emphasized in raising you and who you are today. Write two positive outcomes and one negative outcome. (For example, a positive outcome might be that a parent overemphasized grace and today you are a very loving and accepting individual regardless of personal differences. A negative outcome might be that your parents overemphasized protection and today you struggle with self-confidence when faced with new challenges because you were offered little to no challenge growing up.)

_____

_____

_____

_____

What pathways did your parents use primarily?

_____

_____

_____

_____

Do you see a connection between the walls your parents emphasized and the walls you emphasize as a parent today?

_____

_____

_____

_____

"A Safe House isn't about parenting perfectly. It's about knowing your own story so you can move from parenting reactively to parenting proactively."
Safe House (Waterbrook Multnomah, p. 73)

WITHIN THE FOUR WALLS: QUESTIONS RELATED TO YOUR KIDS

In what ways do you need to better balance the walls of grace and truth in relationship to your kids?

_____

_____

_____

_____

In what ways do you need to better balance the walls of exploration and protection in relationship to your kids?

_____

_____

_____

_____

Remember, if you get this right, even just two out of five times, you're doing well!

What is your "go-to" pathway? Do you see a connection between how you were raised and why this is your "go-to?"

_____

_____

_____

_____

What do you find difficult about veering away from your normal parenting strategy to the Safe House Pathway?

_____

_____

_____

_____

On a scale of 1 to 10, with 10 being extremely well, how often do you apologize to your children for something you did wrong? How specific are you with them about the offense?

_____

_____

_____

_____

Describe the last time you had to apologize to one of your children. How did you make it right with him/her?

_____

_____

_____

BECOMING SAFE: APPLICATION

When you're anxious or your mind is racing this week, go immediately to prayer. Stop what you're doing as soon as you can and journal about your experience.

✔ Go on a date with your spouse to a racquetball, handball or squash court. Pretend the wall you're hitting the ball on is the wall you most need to knock down. As you play together, release the fears you have about erecting the other wall. Afterward, go to dinner together and lay out a plan for how the two of you will begin to balance the four walls with your kids better over time.

✔ Start a give, save, spend jar with your children. Allow them to earn money for certain tasks you assign. Teach them to give the first 10% in the give jar, to save another certain percentage in the save jar and, finally, to take what's left over to spend. This teaches children about the truths of money.

✔ Make a list of the top five values you want your children to inherit. Get them made on a canvas or picture and hang them where you can all see them on a daily basis. Break down each value in respect to the four walls and implement creative ways to instill these values in your children over time (similar to the give, save, spend jar).

✔ Take the Safe House Assessment in *Safe House* to discover your parenting tendencies (Waterbrook Multnomah, p. 88-91). Bring them with you ready to discuss for the next session.

NOTES

NOTES

NOTES

LESSON FOUR:
OUR PARENTING TENDENCIES

INTRODUCTION

THE ONE BEHAVIOR EVERY PARENT MUST STOP DOING

My dad bought my son, Landon, a tee ball set for his second birthday. I admit, **everything in me** wanted him to immediately pick up the bat and ball and start swinging for the fences.

But he didn't. Instead, he wanted to gather stones from our backyard and fill up his Little Tikes® plastic golf bag with them.

No matter how much I tried to make hitting that ball off the tee fun for him, **he couldn't have cared less**! In fact, he didn't care at all.

I was bummed. I love playing baseball. I also wrestled.

Fortunately, my dad **supported me** regardless of my performance on the field or mat. **He definitely challenged me when I didn't do well, but his support came first.**

That wasn't the case for all parents in the stands. I witnessed some ugly interactions between parents and kids on the baseball field and wrestling mat through the years. Cursing. Yelling. Even physical aggression. **Parents who challenged their kids hard, but offered no support.**

No child deserves to be treated this way.

Some of these kids were so incredibly talented they had full Division I college scholarships, *but sadly squanded them*. Anybody with common sense knew why.

Their parents were more invested than they were. So much so, that by the time they got to college, **they were burnt out**.

I use sports as the illustration because it's where you see this behavior in parents the most.

Whether it's their grades, career aspirations, or wishing your kids had a completely different personality, parents have agendas.

But these agendas not only wreck us, they also emotionally debilitate our kids.

That's why the **one behavior every one of us must stop right now is living our own unfulfilled lives through our kids.**

They don't deserve the pressure.

As a dad, I have some soul searching to do. As a counselor, I know the ramifications of unmet expectations at their worst.

I remember meeting with a very insightful young man a few years ago. He was failing out of school, socially using drugs and living a sexually promiscuous lifestyle.

However, it didn't take long to see the pressure this young man was under. His dad was a respectable ministry leader, and his expectations for his son were for him to be the same.

Rather than loving his son for who he was, he shamed him for who he wasn't.

His tearful, heart-wrenching confession is one no child should have to make: *"Josh, my dad's expectations for me are so high, I know I'll never be who he wants me to be."*

How sad.

The Bible tells us to *"train up a child in the way he should go."* Notice the verse emphasizes the way each child should go, not the way we want them to go.

The question I needed to ask myself was, "Will I love my son any less if he doesn't like baseball?"

Of course I wouldn't love him any less. Not from my perspective as dad, anyway.

But I might treat him differently. And though we may not be yelling and swearing at our kids, parents' expectations are expressed over time in subtle messages and attitudes that reveal our agendas.

There are two ways to gauge how strong your parental agenda is for your kids.

> 1. Do you use shame as a motivator against your kids when they don't meet your expectations?

> 2. How well are you becoming a student of your child's interests, especially if they are not interests of your own?

Better yet, what if I privately were to ask your kids, *"Do you feel like your mom (or dad) loves you more (or less) because you play (or don't play) a certain sport, instrument, or some other activity?"*

We all must stop living our unfulfilled lives through our kids.

I want to close with an excerpt from John Smoltz's (former Atlanta Braves pitcher) Hall of Fame induction speech in Cooperstown on July 26, 2015.

In his closing statement, he received loud applause with these words, "I want to encourage families and parents… baseball is not a year-round sport."

He continued:

*"I want to encourage you, if nothing else, know that your children's passion and desire to play baseball is something that they can do without a competitive pitch. Every throw a kid makes today is a competitive pitch. **They don't go outside; they don't have fun; they don't throw enough**. But they're competing and maxing out too hard, too early, and that's why we're having these problems (referring to Tommy John surgery). So please, take care of those great future arms."*

And might I add, "… **those great future hearts**."

Get outside.

Have fun.

Enjoy your kids' interests.

And if they're good enough to one day do whatever it is they love professionally, support their dreams, *not your own*, with all of your heart.

 **VIDEO JOURNAL**

Helicopter Parent: High Grace, High Protection

BFF Parent: High Grace, High Exploration

Religious Parent: High Truth, High Protection

Boss Parent: High Truth, High Exploration

Two ways we parent out of fear:

_____

Perfectionism

_____

Parental Agendas

> *"Train up a child **in the way he should go**; even when*
> *he is old he will not depart from it."*
> Proverbs 22:6, ESV

The story of the Bible includes four major parts: creation, fall of mankind, redemption, and consummation (Christ's Second Coming).

When we see our kids only in light of creation, we tend to see them as God's gift to earth. They are a gift from God, but that's not all. Parents who treat their kids as if that's all they are tend to overemphasize grace and parent from a Helicopter or BFF tendency.

On the other hand, our children, just like us, are fallen, sinful beings. Parents who treat their kids as if that's all they are, however, tend to overemphasize truth and parent from a Religious or Boss tendency.

Instead, seeing our children in light of both creation and the fall allows us the opportunity to teach them about the redemptive work and love of Jesus Christ and balance how we parent.

Write out the tendencies of each parent type and the corresponding messages received by the children.

Helicopter:

_____

_____

BFF:

_____

_____

Religious:

_____

_____

Boss:

_____

_____

The Safe House Parent balances these four walls over time. Recognizing and knowing our tendency is critical to knowing how well to balance the four walls.

Steps for Balancing the Four Walls:

1. Allow your kids, age-appropriately, to experience the natural consequences of their actions.

2. Set age-appropriate limits while staying connected to your child's heart.

3. Don't allow them to explore further than their age permits. Your three-year-old should not be allowed to dictate what he/she eats for dinner, and your nine-year-old doesn't need to stay up until whenever he/she feels tired.

4. Have set consequences for behaviors. Be proactive.

5. Set clear roles, be consistent, and follow through.

6. Sit with them and listen to their day in vulnerable moments. Don't fix their problems; just listen to their feelings about their day.

7. One of the most effective ways of balancing the four walls is giving our children 20 minutes a day of command-free play time. This is where we sit and play with them, entering into their world and doing what they want to do.

For more detailed information on how to set up command-free time, please refer to *Safe House*, Waterbrook Multnomah, p. 78-79.

For more practical ways to balance the four walls, refer to *Safe House*, Waterbrook Multnomah, p. 80, 85-86, 99, and 105.

YOU ARE THE SAFEHOUSE: QUESTIONS FOR YOU

What was your parenting tendency on the Safe House Assessment? Do you agree or disagree with the outcome? Why? What surprised you?

_____
_____
_____
_____

Now that you have an idea of your parenting tendency, write down three new steps you're going to take to balance your four walls?

_____
_____
_____
_____

How does fear reveal itself in how you parent? Through perfectionism? Parental agendas? Criticism toward your kids? Anger? Something else?

_____
_____
_____
_____

What parental agendas are you putting on your child?

_____
_____
_____
_____

What are you most afraid of happening to him/her? Write down and label your insecurities.

_____
_____
_____
_____

Do you find yourself comparing your kids, family life, or status with other parents on social media? How does this impact how you parent your children? What is it about what others are doing that matters so much to you? Why?

_____
_____
_____
_____

Write down how comparison, parental agendas or perfectionism are robbing you of freedom as a parent.

_____

_____

_____

_____

"For freedom Christ has set us free; stand firm therefore,
and do not submit again to a yoke of slavery."
Galatians 5:1, ESV

WITHIN THE FOUR WALLS: QUESTIONS RELATED TO YOUR KIDS

Christi and I had a discussion one evening with her parents about creating a Safe House when her mum read us a passage she used in raising her three children:

"By *wisdom* a house is built,
and by *understanding* it is established;
by *knowledge* the rooms are filled
with all precious and pleasant riches."
Proverbs 24:3-4, ESV (emphasis added)

As I crawled into bed that evening, I couldn't get this verse out of my head. How do we apply wisdom in raising our children?

After a bit of study, I learned the word wisdom in this verse is not a philosophical term, but a practical one. The Hebrew word is used frequently throughout the Old Testament to describe the hands-on work of ants, locusts, and even lizards. Though not all that smart, they are wise by how they live.

To build our house on wisdom is to balance all four walls of a Safe House: exploration, protection, grace, and truth. One way to really know if our narrative is becoming more coherent and healing is to measure how much we're growing in wisdom as parents. Here's a good metric:

"The wisdom from above is first pure, then peaceable, gentle, open to reason,
full of mercy and good fruits, impartial and sincere. And a harvest of righteous-
ness is sown in peace by those who make peace."
James 3:17-19, ESV

These verses are a litmus test for how much we're growing in wisdom and how much our past stories may be impacting our present behavior as parents. If there are kinks in our own stories, we'll know it by the way we're treating our kids. Consider the first characteristic listed: pure. As you interact with your children— no matter their age or circumstance—are you doing so with a pure heart, applying what you know is best for them?

Take a few moments to consider how well you're responding, not reacting, to your anxious, rebellious, and fearful children.

~ Am I approaching my kids—their dirty diapers, skinned knees, spilled milk, late curfew, and disrespectful attitude—in a peaceable manner?

~ Am I approaching my kids when they are in their worst, most fearful, scared, angry, even disrespectful moments in a peaceable manner? Just because our kids disrespect us doesn't mean we should disrespect them back. It's how we model our behavior that matters in terms of whether or not they feel safe.

~ Am I gentle in how I talk to, care for, set limits with, discipline, and help my children? Am I growing in gentleness over time?

~ Am I open to reason with my children when we don't see eye to eye? (Not in matters that compromise my parental authority.)

~ Am I growing in mercy or holding my child's past behaviors against him? Consider Psalm 103:9: "[God the Father] will not always chide."

~ Am I becoming more kind, patient, faithful, good, peaceful, gentle, loving, self-controlled, and joyful toward my kids and my spouse?

~ Am I treating each of our kids individually in our home in the same manner, showing no favoritism?

~ Am I becoming less of a hypocrite, living according to the attitudes and behaviors I expect of my spouse and kids?

Using a scale of 1 to 10, I encourage you to measure yourself according to each of these questions once a month over the next three months. You may even want to give this list to your spouse or children and ask: "Can you help me with this? I want to be a better parent. Next month, we are going to walk through this, and I want you to tell me how I'm doing."

If you don't find yourself improving, it may be a reflection of an unresolved moment in your story. If you need wisdom, the Bible says to simply ask for it. Christi and I pray for wisdom, with our kids present, every night.

(Excerpt taken from *Safe House*, Waterbrook Multnomah, p. 107-108)

BECOMING SAFE: APPLICATION

✔ Sit down with your spouse this week and ask him/her to rate you on each of the questions. Do it again in a month to see how well you're growing in your relationship together.

✔ Sit down with your children and ask them to rate you on each of the questions. Do it again in a month and see how well you're growing in your relationship with them.

✔ Begin blocking off 20 minutes a day this week with your children and enter into command-free playtime together.

✔ Fast from social media this week where you compare yourself to others.

✔ Go on a date with your spouse. Find an activity neither one of you are very good at and attempt it together. For instance, you could go roller-skating, ice skating, kayaking, tandem biking, etc. As you do this activity together, think about ways you can get better. Parallel it with where you need to improve in your parenting tendency. Go to dinner afterward and talk about each of your parenting tendencies and begin putting a plan together to balance one another and the four walls as parents.

✔ Find an activity your child absolutely loves doing, especially if it's something you don't like or know a lot about, and enter his/her world. Have your child teach you about that activity. Be invested in it and help support your child to discover his/her strengths.

NOTES

NOTES

NOTES

LESSON FIVE: SAFE DISCIPLINE

INTRODUCTION

3 WAYS TO MAKE DISCIPLINE EASIER

"Sit up to the table in your chair, Landon. It's time for dinner," I said cheerfully.

Not a millisecond later came that boisterous and very powerful word from our defiant two-year-old,

"No!"

No?!

What happened to the sweet, innocent boy I used to rock to sleep? Our compliant little (I mean, big) eater who always responded enthusiastically when food was put in front of him? For crying out loud, this is a boy whose favorite food at nine months was spinach and feta frittata!

Now I'm wondering who this kid is. And why he's calling me "Dad."

I'm not sure of your bent, but I tend to err on the side of permissiveness to make life a bit easier in moments like these. **Because sometimes our angry reaction to our children is worse than allowing them to behave the way they are.**

> However, permissiveness cannot be our default mode, lest we raise children who have little understanding of life's consequences.

This is why Landon's defiance and how we remain consistent in disciplining him is the dominating topic of Christi's and my conversation.

On this particular Saturday, I was feeling the weight of it.

Hoping to enjoy playtime together, I spent the entire morning "guiding" him—mostly to the corner. He wouldn't listen to anything I asked.

Me: "Okay, time for a diaper change."

L: "No!"

Me: "Sit up in your chair to eat."

L: "No!"

Me: "Give Kennedy her toy back."

L: "No!"

By the time I got him down for a nap, I felt relieved he was finally in bed and disappointed with how our morning went.

Sitting down for a quick break, I stumbled upon a phrase I'd read many times, only this time it jumped out at me like I hadn't remembered before—a sentence that freed me the rest of the afternoon.

Discipline "rescues children from the 'tyranny of their own desires.'"

I don't know about you but, to me, that's an eye-opener. I write and speak a lot about the culture we're raising our kids in, a culture that values feeling better over loving better. Kids today caught up more in loving #selfies than loving others.

> Giving in to our children's desires as our default mode to keep them happy or compliant keeps them enslaved to the "tyranny of their own desires." To put it bluntly, such kids are most likely to become selfish, entitled brats at best, full- blown addicts at worst.

Later that Saturday afternoon, Christi and I took both kids for a walk in their 21st century Radio Flyer® wagon. As we talked about the morning, we reframed the importance of rough starts like we had earlier that day. I put them here into three ways of thinking about discipline that makes it a bit easier on us all.

1. Our kids' "no" is a healthy move toward interdependence.

Children are trying to find their identities independently from their parents, even as early as two years of age. **This is a good thing**. Otherwise, we would raise compliant robots who never develop an identity of their own. So the next time your toddler or preschooler says "no," **celebrate** that he/she is becoming his/her own little person with independent, big thoughts and ideas about the world. *Then count to 10 slowly*.

The word "no" is also a gem because our children begin to learn that not only are they using it to set boundaries, but so are others. **There's no better time** to teach kids how to set boundaries and learn empathy than from the moment they start saying "no." **There's also no better place** to learn how to interact with the boundaries set by others than in the safety of their own homes with your guidance.

Besides, saying "no" as an adult is one of the healthiest words to determine our relational, emotional, and occupational success.

2. Kids who learn to willfully choose the right behaviors (rather than always being forced into them or allowed out of them) **develop self-control**.

Children are not born into the world distinguishing between right and wrong and what is good or bad for them. Because of that, they will misbehave—a lot. They will likely prefer ice cream over broccoli, jumping on the couch to sitting still, and coloring on the walls in place of a coloring book.

Instead of thinking about how we get our children to behave in a given situation, we need to think about how we get our children to choose their behavior. There's a difference. The first leads to compliance, the latter leads to thoughtful consideration of how their behavior influences others.

Here's the good news: This only takes about 20 years.

Just the other night Christi was getting ready to take Landon to the park where I was playing softball in a local church league. Thinking it would be fun for the whole family, she really wanted to go too. However, because of Landon's misbehavior, getting out the door was a fiasco.

Christi knew by taking Landon to the park she would be giving in to him. So she stayed home with him explaining that it was because of his choice to not "stop and listen" that they were unable to go to the park.

When I got him out of bed the next morning, his first words to me were, *"Mommy sad. Landon sad. No park."*

Though Christi paid the price that night, it was a parenting win.

3. Discipline is not a short-term technique; it's a long-term posture.

Raising kids who live, love, and lead well is teaching our children to choose between right and wrong actions and select friends, foods, and behaviors that are good for them, not bad. But doing so doesn't happen overnight.

Expecting kids to make good decisions at such young ages can cause a lot of frustration—until we realize what a privilege it is to be our children's primary teacher (discipline means "to train") for the first 18+ years of their lives. Lowering these expectations a bit is helpful because doing so allows us to celebrate the special moments when they make great decisions on their own.

And that's what we want to reinforce.

If we get caught up in, disappointed about, and beat ourselves up over the "wasted" Saturday mornings, we'll miss the big picture—that what we're really trying to do with the years our children live under our roofs is "rescue them from the tyranny of their own desires."

Besides, as adults, isn't that what our Heavenly Father is trying to do with us when He says "no?"

 VIDEO JOURNAL

Punishment and discipline are different. Simply put, punishment isn't safe; discipline is. In punishment, we *react* to misbehavior; in discipline, we *respond* to it. The short-term outcome of punishment may be obedience; but the long-term outcome of discipline is self-discipline.

When we punish our kids, shame, guilt, criticism, and contempt become the posture from which we parent. As one parenting expert reflects, "Where did we ever get the crazy idea that in order to make children do better, first we have to make them feel worse? Think of the last time you felt humiliated or treated unfairly. Did you feel like cooperating or doing better?"[ix] Remember, punishment focuses purely on behavior and lacks grace for the child. As a consequence, our kids may be well-behaved in the short-term, but they lack the skills or the self-worth to make wise decisions in the long run.

Discipline, on the other hand, is postured in both grace and truth. Derived from the Latin root *disciplina*, the word means to educate and instruct, to teach and to guide. Safe discipline, at its core, is about skill-building—developing our child's internal moral compass and equipping her with the self-discipline necessary to make wise choices when we're not around. As H.L. Mencken famously observed, "Morality is doing what's right, no matter what you're told. Obedience is doing what you're told, no matter what's right."

(Excerpted from *Safe House*, Waterbrook Multnomah, p. 111-112)

> *"Fathers, don't exasperate your children by coming down hard on them. Take them by the hand and lead them in the way of the Master."*
> Ephesians 6:4, MSG

Read Ephesians 6:4. Whereas exasperation emotionally stirs up our kids, the word *admonition* used in this verse means "counsel," and refers to "placing the mind in a proper place" as to *"reason"* with our kids by warning them (admonishing). In real-people language, this verse instructs parents to become counselors to our child, and through our nurturing, calm her brain so that she's able to reason with us and problem solve for the solution that will best honor God.

> That's discipline: *being emotionally safe, taking our children by the hand, and lovingly re-directing them.*

(Excerpted from *Safe House*, Waterbrook Multnomah, p. 112)

The difficulty of safe discipline:

> *"We love because he first loved us."*
> 1 John 4:19, ESV

Opening the Door is when we see every emotion—especially difficult emotions like sadness and anger—as an opportunity to connect. Here is where we empathize with our children's feelings.

(For more on Opening the Door, see *Safe House*, Waterbrook Multnomah, p. 114-117.)

Moving to Another Room is when we address the behavior. Where opening the door is leading with grace, moving to another room is where we implement the truth.

For little ones, Moving to Another Room is a literal strategy. For most toddlers, there's one word that will become your best friend—*distraction*. We literally take them into another room and distract them from their meltdowns.
(For more on Moving to Another Room for Little Ones, see *Safe House*, Waterbrook Multnomah, p. 117-120.)

For older children and teenagers, Moving to Another Room is a figurative strategy.

Starting roughly around the age of eight, there's a big jump in our child's ability to think rationally. No longer is moral development about rewards and consequences or how behavior impacts only one person. Children begin to learn how everyone is impacted by decisions and are able to start problem solving with less influence from us on directing behavior.

(For more on Moving to Another Room for Older Ones, see *Safe House*, Waterbrook Multnomah, p. 120-125.)

Empathy is when we allow our children to express their concerns without jumping to conclusions or being judgmental. This doesn't mean we agree with their feelings or beliefs. Empathy means we listen well and see the situation from our children's perspective.

Assertiveness is when we state our concerns without personally attacking our children. "You always," "you never," "I can't believe you would…" are not helpful here. Never attack character.

Respect can be difficult, but critical to building a Safe House. Respect means we refuse to be mean and nasty even if our children are being mean and nasty to us. Respect also means we refuse to judge our children or assume the worst about them.

Building a Fence is when we problem solve together with our children and teenagers to find a solution.

Inviting our children to help us make a decision is critical for connection and brain growth. Whenever possible, the more situations we invite our children to problem solve together, the more they learn to weigh consequences and make wise decisions in the future.

Collaboration with our children to determine limits, and the consequences, helps them experience the realities and boundaries of life. They can also come back to the drawing board to reevaluate a solution that may not have worked out for the best. Doing so provides incredible teaching moments for us as parents, but also unites us with our children in raising them to live, love, and lead well.

> *"I think of discipline as the continual everyday process of helping a child learn self-discipline."*
> Fred Rogers

SOME PRINCIPLES FOR SAFE DISCIPLINE:

✔ If your children feel a rupture in the relationship with you over what they did, that can be the strongest consequence a child receives. If they feel remorse for what they did, allow that to be enough.

✔ Give your kids a mulligan.

✔ Give your child opportunities to make you proud. Use rewards for positive reinforcement and consequences for negative reinforcement.

✔ **Set clear rules. Be consistent. Follow through.

If you don't know what the rules are as a parent, you can't expect your kids to know them either.

✔ Ask "what" questions. In approaching a defiant child, try to use "what" questions, not "why" questions. Just like adults, kids experience "why" questions as criticism, putting them on the defensive: "Why did you just say that?" "Why can't you calm down?" "Why can't you be more like your sister?" Instead, ask "what" questions: "What was going on that got you so upset?" "What did you need?" "What were you feeling?"

✔ Use educated guesses when your child says, "I don't know."

(For more Nuts and Bolts of Safe Discipline, see *Safe House*, Waterbrook Mult-nomah, p. 118-120 and 124-125.)

YOU ARE THE SAFE HOUSE: QUESTIONS FOR YOU

Describe where you've had the most difficulty as it relates to discipline.

_____
_____
_____
_____

What did you learn in this lesson that can help you with that difficulty?

_____
_____
_____
_____

In what areas do you and your spouse need to be more consistent when it comes to discipline?

_____
_____
_____
_____

WITHIN THE FOUR WALLS: QUESTIONS RELATED TO YOUR KIDS

As you discipline your kids, ask yourself, "Am I responding in the emotionally safest way possible? What is going on within them right now that is causing them to behave this way?"

_____
_____
_____
_____

What discipline strategies do your children respond to best? Do you see a difference in how your children respond to certain strategies?

_____
_____
_____
_____

How did the Ephesians 6:4 passage change the way you think about disciplining your children?

_____
_____
_____
_____

Write down the two most exhausting parts of discipline for you.

_____
_____
_____
_____

What three, new strategies did you learn in this lesson that you're going to apply this week?

_____
_____
_____
_____

BECOMING SAFE: APPLICATION

✔ Practice Empathy, Assertiveness, and Respect with your spouse this week. Find a situation you don't agree on, listen to your spouse's concern with empathy, state your concern once your spouse feels understood, and do it all in respect. Then, collaborate on a solution.

✔ Take two of the discipline strategies you learned in this lesson and apply them this week with your kids. Journal about how you feel doing them. How are your kids responding?

✔ When your child listens well this week, celebrate big time! Take him/her for ice cream, go to a park or favorite store together and pick out a new toy. Too often, we veer toward constant consequences and negative moods. Learn to celebrate well when your kids are living out the values you want to see in them. Practice that this week.

✔ We don't have the capacity to love without first experiencing the love of God for us (1 John 4:19). When you're exhausted this week over inconsistent behavior or discipline issues with your kids, practice waking up 30 minutes prior to everyone in the house. If you have to go to bed 30 minutes earlier this week, do it. Nothing will rejuvenate your ability to be present and problem solve with your kids more than getting into the Truth each day.

NOTES

NOTES

LESSON SIX:
RAISING KIDS WHO LOVE WELL

INTRODUCTION

3 WORDS OUR KIDS NEED US TO BELIEVE

We were at dinner a few months back with our dear friends, Adam and Stephanie. They have a son, Aiden, only three months older than our son, Landon. These boys have been best buddies since the day they were born.

Okay, I confess, with the friendship Adam and I have, **they don't have much of a choice.**

I remember walking out from dinner that night beside Adam, who was carrying Aiden on his shoulders. Landon held my hand beside me.

On our way through the parking lot, I heard Adam ask, *"Aiden, whose got it?"* Aiden emphatically shouted, *"God's got it!"*

Now you see why Christi and I trust our son with these friends. On our way home that night, I started teaching Landon the same principle—**that no matter the circumstances in our lives, we can trust that God's got it.**

However, this lesson didn't go quite as smoothly in the Straub household. Every night I put Landon down to bed in the weeks following, I would ask him, "Whose got it?"

   "Whandon's got it!" he would cheerfully say.

Not once could I get him to say, *"God's got it!"*

Confused, I asked Christi one day why she thought he kept doing that. That's when the light bulb went on, "Josh" she said, *"Every time I ask him to do a task around the house, I'll encourage him by saying, 'You can do this; you got it buddy.'"*

Hence, Landon's got it.

We tried a few more times after that, but the saying slowly faded as we simply jumped right into our nighttime prayers for the next few months.
Until about two weeks ago—at the dinner table.

We were going through some pretty difficult times that had me **more stressed and anxious than I am comfortable admitting**. With so much going on, Landon and I sat down for dinner while Christi tended to Kennedy in another room.

Focused on my dinner, I was clearly not my normal self with Landon that night, because out of nowhere, while eating his own dinner, he nonchalantly says, **"God's got it, dad."**

> What?! I couldn't believe it. The first time our two-year-old said, "*God's got it,*" is **to me, not for me**—perhaps to tell me that if I'm going to teach it to him, I'd better live it too.

I'm not sure if he intended that, but it worked.

And truth be told, all of the anxiety I had about the situation was finally resolved in a way that only God could have pulled off.

> Yes, Landon, *God's got it.*

Since that night, I've learned two reasons why our kids need us to believe those three simple words:

1. The biggest culprit to being emotionally present and enjoying playful moments with our kids is worry.

> When we're worried, our brains go into fight or flight mode, causing us to fixate on what we're anxious about. **The more attention we give the fear, the less we give to our kids.**

> Simply put, ***worry robs us from the joyful moments of play our kids crave from us***.

2. No matter what you're going through right now, God's got it.

Do you trust Him?

Or, for the piece of humble pie I received, here's a better question: *If I asked your kids if you trust God, what would they tell me?*

 **VIDEO JOURNAL**

Wishing your marriage on your kids.

Our home should be the emotionally safest place on the planet for our spouses.

Use feeling words to describe your day with your spouse.
The marital relationship is the one God uses to describe His union in the Trinity—a relationship that is the direct reflection of the Godhead itself. Our marriage is a foundation for raising kids with a faith that sticks.

Raising kids who leave a spiritual legacy.

Write steadfast love of the tablet of your kids' hearts.

Using Moses' wisdom, here are the "magic moments" of the day where our faith spills over into the hearts of our kids.

- **Eating meals together.** It's an unbelievably optimal time to have focused discussion with your kids about their day, feelings, friends, and failings. Start eating together as a family—try to begin with at least five meals a week with your kids. No technology.

- **Walking or traveling together.** Moses refers to it as "walking along the road." We refer to it as "drive time." As you drive around town taking your kids to school and extracurricular activities, power-down the technology. There will be many days nobody says a word, but your presence with your kids during this time opens up the opportunity for the one conversation that could matter.

- **Tucking kids into bed.** Don't send your kids off to bed on their own. Fight the urge to turn on the T.V. or tackle the kitchen clean up. Take time to walk them there and tuck them in. There is something special about the private domain of a child's bedroom that allows a kid to be vulnerable. You never know when you'll be called upon to be your child's counselor in these precious moments.

• **Getting up in the morning provides a blank page for families to get a fresh start.** Make it a point every morning—whether it's sticking a note in Emma's lunch box, thanking Luke for cleaning up the kitchen, or spending an extra few minutes to read a book to Parker—to give your kids the spiritual energy they need for whatever happens to them that day.

How much do you believe that praying for your children matters? Here's a quick litmus test: **Ask yourself how often you pray for and with them.**

Here are three ideas to get started:

1. Pray *with* your kids.
We pray with Landon every night before bed. We ask him who he wants to pray for. Sometimes he answers us. Other times he just listens. As part of the routine each night, he asks us to read the verse hanging over his bed.

"The Lord your God is with you. He is mighty to save. He will take great delight in you. He will quiet you with his love. He will rejoice over you with singing."
Zephaniah 3:17, NIV

I hope our children learn the importance of praying Scripture.

2. Pray *for* your kids.
One of my closest friends, Adam Donyes, has a son a few months older than Landon. Our little guys are also quickly becoming good buddies.

Adam told me he bought a Bible designed similar to a journal he was reading from cover to cover. The purpose was to read the entire Bible and write prayers specifically for, and to, his son in the journal sections as he is prompted to pray them. When his son is 18-years-old, he will bury it in the mountains of Colorado, give his son a map and, as a rite of passage, have his son discover that Bible.

I chose to do the same thing. And both of us are praying prayers for our sons we never thought we'd pray.

I hope our children learn these prayers for them are timeless.

3. *Circle* your kids in prayer.
Christi and I pray circles around our kids based on Mark Batterson's book, *The Circle Maker*. We circle prayers for our kids' spouses, health, education, and especially their faith development and character. One of Batterson's insights has stuck with me. He wrote, "Our prayers never die." You can pray today for your great, great, great grandkids and those prayers won't die with you.

(Excerpted from *Safe House*, Waterbrook Multnomah, p. 194-195)

Kids need a group of people who believe in them and will instill the same faith values in the same way we do as parents in our homes.

Kids need four key influences:

• A Safe House of immediate family.
As parents, establishing faith means we prioritize heavenly matters, not earthly success in our homes. Living in a culture of busyness, it's too easy to fall victim ourselves, filling our kids' schedules with activities that build their grades, athletic prowess, or musical talent, while allowing spiritual growth to become an afterthought. Jesus says it's no good to allow our kids to gain the whole world, yet forfeit their soul (Mark 8:36).

> Full calendars cannot replace empty souls.

• A Safe House of extended family.
These adults either are or become like extended family to our children. They include at least three or four other adults who function as the child's "faith team" outside of the parents—aunts, uncles, grandparents, mentors, or any other supporting cast. I encourage singles to become aunts and uncles to other families to help parents have date nights. I also encourage spiritually and emotionally healthy men to mentor fatherless kids.

• A Safe House tribe of social relationships.
We are who we spend time with. The Bible says "bad company corrupts good character" (1 Corinthians 15:33, ESV). Here's where coaches, teachers, pastors, and other parents support our children to reinforce the values we're teaching in the home.

• Intergenerational activities and worship with great-grandparents, grandparents, and parents. Research shows that intergenerational worship promotes a faith that sticks[x]. We pick our children up from their classrooms immediately following the sermon so they can worship with us in the main sanctuary to close out the service. These moments of worshipping with our kids create sweet memories and provide meaningful conversation for those ordinary moments, like bedtime.

(Excerpted from *Safe House*, Waterbrook Multnomah, p. 196-197)

> *The more kid-centered the home, the more unsafe the marriage.*
> *I know kids can be all-consuming, but an inability to pay attention*
> *to your spouse's heart will wreak havoc on your children.*
> *Safe House* (Waterbrook Multnomah, p. 176)

YOU ARE THE SAFE HOUSE: QUESTIONS FOR YOU

From your perspective, what are your kids learning about love and romance based on your marriage? What are they learning about how to treat the opposite sex?

_____
_____
_____
_____

In the spirit of Hebrews 13:4, write down ways you can begin honoring marriage in front of your kids. What applications from this lesson do you most look forward to doing?

_____
_____
_____
_____

Write down the one area of your marriage you don't want to wish on your kids. What next step are you going to take to make that area more desirable for your kids?

_____
_____
_____
_____

Write down two aspects of your marriage you would wish on your kids.

_____
_____
_____
_____

Knowing that our kids do as we do more than as we say, how do you need to begin treating your spouse differently in front of them?

_____
_____
_____
_____

Describe your relationship with God.

_____
_____
_____
_____

Knowing that our kids do as we do more than as we say, how do you need to begin interacting with God differently to show your kids you love and trust Him?

_____
_____
_____
_____

What limits or boundaries on technology do you need to set in your life? In your marriage?

_____
_____
_____
_____

Who is on your Safe Life Team? If you don't yet have one, who could you consider asking to be a part of it? What step will you take this week to build one?

_____
_____
_____
_____

WITHIN THE FOUR WALLS: QUESTIONS RELATED TO YOUR KIDS

In the spirit of Hebrews 13:4, write down three ways you can begin to honor your children's future marriages.

Who, or what, has the most influence right now on the tablet of your kids' hearts? What are some ways you can begin to help your children write steadfast love on the tablet of their hearts?

_____
_____
_____
_____

What limits or boundaries on technology do you need to set with your kids?

_____
_____
_____
_____

Which mundane moment of the day described by Moses do you need to begin paying more attention to for the heart of your child? How will you begin doing that this week?

_____
_____

_____

_____

Write down one way you can begin to make prayer matter in the lives of your kids beginning this week.

_____

_____

_____

_____

In the 21st century, we have to be vigilant about who our kids are spending time with and what they're doing. How much time have you spent getting to know the people who speak into your kids' lives—their teachers, coaches, and leaders at your local church? How strategic are you about inviting them over for dinner to get to know who they are? Do you know the friends your kids spend the most time with? How well do you know their parents? What can you do this week to begin getting to know them all better?

_____

_____

_____

_____

BECOMING SAFE: APPLICATION

✔ Begin praying for your children's spouses. Pray, too, that God protects their eyes, hearts, minds and souls from sexual perversion and relational gluttony.

✔ Instead of numbing yourself in a heartless device that cares nothing about your relationships, carve out 15 minutes of your evening with your spouse each night this week and do two things:

1. Inquire about your spouse's heart.
Literally ask the questions, "What's on your heart today?" "How are you feeling?" Make it a priority to not fix anything! Just sit with your spouse, with no condemnation, and listen to his/her most prevalent feelings from the day. Don't fix it; just validate it.

2. Then, share your heart with your spouse.
Use feeling words to describe your day. "I felt sad when…" or "I felt angry at…" Simply using feeling words engages both sides of the brain and strengthens our bonds with others.

Practice this for 15 minutes, even if it's just a few times a week. The investment is worth it—both for you and your kids. When Christi and I are in survival mode and find ourselves becoming insensitive toward one another, these are the steps we use to reunite. Practice them often.

✔ **Get Away Together.** Christi and I take a date night once a week, just the two of us. Even if you cannot do this once a week, try every other week. Some of our favorite memories together are just dropping the kids off at our adopted grandparents' house, then coming home, putting on PJ's, ordering food in, and watching a movie. Sometimes we do game nights at a local coffee shop. Whatever the date, it doesn't have to be extravagant—it just has to be together.

If you struggle finding time to be creative with your dates or live in the middle of nowhere with limited options, my pastor, Ted Cunningham, and I created 10 date night ideas around certain themes like play, laugh, dream, curiosity, and adventure. Not only do they provide creative date night ideas, but they also have 52 questions for each date night to help trigger conversation.

You can download these date nights free at www.joshuastraub.com/members.

✔ **Experience the Joy of the Moment.** The mundane can be a tough place to live. However, it's in the mundane that I've seen my son kiss his baby sister any time he hears her crying. It's also in the mundane at 4:30 a.m. that my baby daughter and I have had our sweetest moments together—cooing, smiling, and praying.

These are also the everyday, ordinary moments that simply make you smile and appreciate the affection you have for your spouse. Christi has this little dance she does that's absolutely adorable to me. On days she breaks into that dance, I simply smile, walk over to her when she's finished, and embrace the moment.

I think many of us miss joy because we are waiting for something extraordinary to happen. One research study[xi] looked at widows and widowers. Without exception, every participant mentioned the mundane moments they remembered most about their spouses.

"If I could just walk back downstairs every morning and see my husband reading the newspaper at the kitchen table, drinking his cup of coffee."

"My wife used to send me crazy text messages throughout the day. I would do anything to get one of those text messages again."

Even when you're frustrated, stressed, and tired, embrace the small moments. Write them down later. And try to fight the urge to pull out your phone. This is a tough one for all of us, but the moment you do, you move from being a participant in the memory to an observer.

Many of my best memories are captured in my heart and mind, not on my phone.

(Excerpted from *Safe House*, Waterbrook Multnomah, p. 180)

As you build a #SafeHouseFamily in the community where you live, be sure to use your membership site for this book and study: http://www.joshuastraub.com/members.

We have a host of creative ideas and resources. Be sure to also join the community of parents using #SafeHouseFamily when posting to social networks to share how you're building a Safe House community.

The more we unite as parents and offer support to one another, the safer our homes will be. The safer our homes are, the stronger our communities will be. And the stronger our communities are, the stronger and safer the society we leave to our kids will be.

That's a legacy worth leaving—together.

#SafeHouseFamily Members: www.joshuastraub.com/members

NOTES

NOTES

APPENDIX:
COUNSELING REFERRALS

If you discover that you need professional counseling beyond the scope of this resource, you can contact your local church for a referral to a licensed professional in your area or use one of the referral sources below:

American Association of Christian Counselors: http://www.aacc.net/resources/find-a-counselor/

Focus on the Family: http://www.focusonthefamily.com/counseling/find-a-counselor.aspx

eCounseling.com: www.ecounseling.com

ABOUT THE AUTHOR

Joshua Straub, Ph.D., is an author, speaker, family advocate and professor of child development. He is the president and cofounder of The Connextion Group, a company designed to empower parents, spouses and families. Josh speaks and writes on emotionally safe parents and spouses and the influence of technology on today's family. He is the author of *Safe House: How Emotional Safety is the Key to Raising Kids Who Live, Love, and Lead Well* and, along with his wife, Christi, is the producer and co-author of the video curriculum, *The Screen-Balanced Family: Six Secrets to a More Connected Family in the 21st Century*. Josh and his Canadian wife, Christi, reside in Nashville, TN, with their son, Landon, and daughter, Kennedy.

NOTES

i Oxford University Dictionary. Oxford University Press.

ii Siegel, D.J. (2007). *The mindful brain: Reflection and attunement in the cultivation of well being* (New York: Norton), 206 (emphasis added).

iii Hoffman, K., Marvin, R., Cooper, G. & Powell, B. (2006). Changing toddlers' and preschoolers' attachment classifications: The Circle of Security Intervention. *Journal of Consulting and Clinical Psychology*, 74, 1017-1026. More information on the circle of security can be found at www.circleofsecurity.org.

iv Siegel, D.J. & Bryson, T.P. (2014). *No-drama discipline: The whole-brain way to calm the chaos and nurture your child's developing mind* (New York: Bantam), xxiv.

v Gottman, J. & DeClaire, J. (1997). *The heart of parenting: How to raise an emotionally intelligent child* (New York: Simon & Schuster).

vi Gottman, J. (2013). "Emotion Coaching: The Heart of Parenting," http://emotioncoaching.gottman.com/about.

vii Negreiros, J. & Miller, L. (2014). The role of parenting in childhood anxiety: Etiological factors and treatment implications. *Clinical Psychology: Science and Practice*, 21(1), 3-17.

viii Laissez-faire parents. *Child development reference*, 5. Retrieved from: http://social.jrank.org/pages/352/Laissez-Faire-Parents.html#ixzz3MkmsXH00.

ix Nelsen, J. (2007). *Positive discipline: The first three years*. New York: Random House, xxi.

x Powell, K. & Clark, C. (2011). *Sticky faith: Everyday ideas to build lasting faith in your kids*. Grand Rapids, MI: Zondervan.

xi Brown, B. (2013). *Daring greatly: How the courage to be vulnerable transforms the way we live, love, parent, and lead*. New York, NY: Gotham Books.

NOTES

NOTES

NOTES

NOTES

NOTES

NOTES